Collins

Primary Social Studies for Antigua and Barbuda

WORKBOOK
GRADE 1

Anthea S Thomas

William Collins' dream of knowledge for all began with the publication of his first book in 1819.
A self-educated mill worker, he not only enriched millions of lives, but also founded a flourishing publishing house. Today, staying true to this spirit, Collins books are packed with inspiration, innovation and practical expertise. They place you at the centre of a world of possibility and give you exactly what you need to explore it.

Collins. Freedom to teach.

Published by Collins
An imprint of HarperCollins*Publishers*
The News Building
1 London Bridge Street
London SE1 9GF

HarperCollins*Publishers*
Macken House,
39/40 Mayor Street Upper,
Dublin 1, D01 C9W8,
Ireland

Browse the complete Collins Caribbean catalogue at
www.collins.co.uk/caribbeanschools

© HarperCollins*Publishers* Limited 2020
Maps © Collins Bartholomew Limited 2020, unless otherwise stated

10 9 8 7 6 5

ISBN 978-0-00-840286-0

British Library Cataloguing-in-Publication Data
A catalogue record for this publication is available from the British Library.

Author: Anthea S. Thomas
Publisher: Elaine Higgleton
In-house senior editor: Julianna Dunn
Development & copy editor: Sue Chapple
Proof reader: Mitch Fitton
Cover designers: Kevin Robbins and Gordon MacGilp
Cover image: Steve Evans
Typesetter: QBS
Illustrator: Danielle Boodoo-Fortuné
Production controller: Lyndsey Rogers
Printed and Bound in the UK by Ashford Colour Press Ltd

MIX
Paper | Supporting
responsible forestry
FSC™ C007454

This book contains FSC™ certified paper and other controlled sources to ensure responsible forest management.

For more information visit: www.harpercollins.co.uk/green

Acknowledgements

The publishers wish to thank the following for permission to reproduce photographs. Every effort has been made to trace copyright holders and to obtain their permission for the use of copyright materials. The publishers will gladly receive any information enabling them to rectify any error or omission at the first opportunity.
(t = top, c = centre, b = bottom, l = left, r = right)

p6tl: Jacob Lund/SS, p6tc: Gelpi/SS, p6tr: Shutterstock, p6bl: Duplass/SS, p6bc: sirtravelalot/SS, p6br: wavebreakmedia/SS, p8: Shutterstock, p19: sylv1rob1/SS, p20tl: Idea tank/SS, p20tc: studiolab/SS, p20tr: Sibrikov Valery/SS, p20bl: Barbara Ash/SS, p20br: He2/SS, p25tl: Editors own, p25tc, 28t: XiXinXing/SS, p25tr: Shutterstock, p25bl: Jacob Lund/SS, p25br, 28b: michaeljung/SS, p39l: Rawpixel.com/SS, p39r: Matyas Rehak/SS, p54t: Quad Design/SS, p54c: Designer things/SS, p54b: phive/SS, p57: Andrey_Popov/SS.
Vectors: Shutterstock

Contents

1 All about me

Student's Book pages 4–15

1 Fill in the gaps in the shapes to describe yourself.

My name is _____.

I am a _____.

I am _____ years old.

I like _____

and _____.

I have _____ eyes.

I have _____ hair.

I am _____.

I am good at

_____

_____

_____.

I live in _____.

2 Draw lines to match the children with the things they are good at.

| Reading | Swimming | Dancing |

| Skipping | Jumping | Riding |

3 One of these is NOT a basic right of a child. Put a circle around it.

To have a name

To be safe

To drink

To have an education

To say how you feel

To have a pet

4 Fill in the missing letters to show the members of the family.

Br __ th __ r   Gr __ ndpa   Fat __ __ r

C __ __ sin

Unc __ __

Gra __ d __ a   Mo __ __ er

5 Read these statements. Are they true or false? Tick the correct box.

	True	False
a Families get smaller when babies are born.	☐	☐
b Families get smaller when people die.	☐	☐
c Death is a happy occasion.	☐	☐
d Birth is a sad occasion.	☐	☐

6 How do you help at home? Finish the sentence in as many ways as you can.

At home I help by ...

- _____
- _____
- _____
- _____
- _____

7 Fill in the blank spaces about your family. Draw pictures of members of your family. Add a word in each space to say who they are.

This is my family

This is me.

This is my _____ .

This is my _____ .

This is my _____ .

This is my _____ .

This is my _____ .

This is my _____ .

This is my _____ .

There are _____ members in my family.

8 On the map, draw in and colour these places to give an idea of your neighbourhood.

| church | school | supermarket | house | clinic |

9 Write the name of each place under the correct picture.

> **police station**   **supermarket**   **school**
> **post office**   **fire station**   **playground**   **church**

_____   _____   _____   _____

_____   _____   _____

10 Write in the name of your village or town in the correct place on the map of Antigua and Barbuda. Draw and colour your house in the box below.

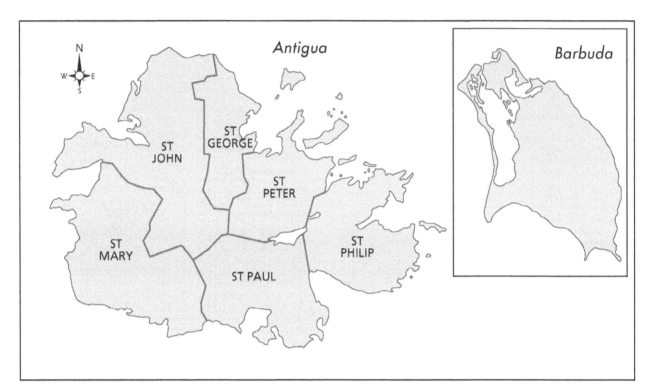

11 Find these words in the puzzle.

BOY
DADDY
EYES
FAMILY
GIRL
HAIR

HELPFUL
KIND
MOMMY
MYSELF
NEIGHBOUR

N	B	P	H	F	R	D	I	X	X
Y	O	C	E	L	U	A	Q	X	R
C	Y	G	L	E	O	D	L	Y	S
C	Z	O	P	S	B	D	G	O	A
Y	B	X	F	Y	H	Y	I	A	I
R	M	E	U	M	G	M	R	M	S
P	I	M	L	A	I	L	L	E	K
J	U	A	O	T	E	H	Y	I	Y
Z	S	C	H	M	N	E	N	V	U
F	A	M	I	L	Y	D	H	T	C

2 Our culture

Student's Book pages 16–27

1 What are the different nationalities in your community? Write as many of them as you can in the box below.

2 Match each group with the thing they are famous for. Draw lines.

Chinese

Syrians

Guyanese

Jamaicans

Antiguans and Barbudans

shawarma

curry roti

fried rice

reggae music

pepperpot

3 What traditions does your family have? Add them to the diagram below.

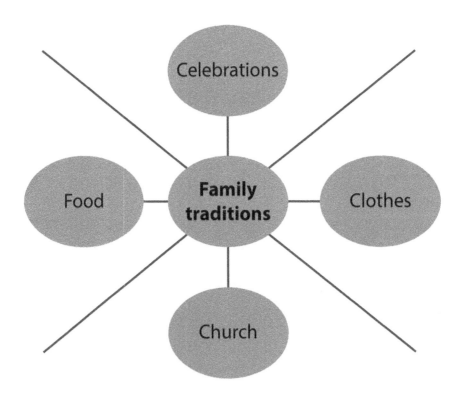

4 Look at this picture.

a What special event does it show?

_____

b Name two things that happen at that event.

_____

_____

5 Name two national festivals that take place each year in Antigua and Barbuda.

_____

_____

6 Circle the utensils used long ago.

7 Choose words from the box to fill in the gaps in the sentences.

> **national anthem**   **different**   **obey**   **get along**

a People need to _____ with each other.

b Everybody is _____ .

c We need to _____ the rules of our community.

d We stand for the _____ _____ .

8 Role-play.

In groups of four, make up a story about children who fall out in the playground. You can act it out for your class. Make sure the children sort out their problem to be friends again!

You can make some notes in the box.

9 Find these words in the puzzle.

BIRTHDAY

CELEBRATE

CULTURE

DANCE

FESTIVAL

FOOD

MUSIC

PAST

RELIGION

WEDDING

E	Z	G	T	R	A	O	D	B	V
L	T	R	E	N	C	C	M	I	G
H	A	A	C	I	S	U	M	R	N
E	F	V	R	X	A	Y	D	T	I
S	C	D	I	B	K	X	O	H	D
M	A	N	I	T	E	R	O	D	D
D	O	M	A	D	S	L	F	A	E
P	A	S	T	D	Y	E	E	Y	W
C	U	L	T	U	R	E	F	C	S
R	E	L	I	G	I	O	N	J	J

3 What do we need?

Student's Book pages 28–43

1 Put a ✓ in the box if it is a need and an ✗ if it is a want.

> ✓ = need   ✗ = want

☐ water

☐ mobile phone

☐ ice-cream

☐ fruit and vegetables

☐ doll

☐ home

☐ air

☐ clothes

2 Use words from the box to fill in the gaps.

water	food	family	survive
money	shelter	fruit	eggs

a Basic needs are things we need in order to _____ .

b Our basic needs are food, _____ clothing, air and

_____ .

c Our _____ provides our basic needs.

d Our parents get _____ from the work that they do.

e Money is used to buy things like _____ .

f Some families grow their own food. They grow _____
and vegetables, and may keep animals for meat, milk and

_____ .

3 Look at the pictures of the community workers. Use a word from the box to name each one on the line below.

> hairdresser   mechanic   nurse
>
> shopkeeper   chef

_____

_____

4 Match the tools to the workers.

Mechanic

Nurse

Hairdresser

Shopkeeper

Chef

5 Draw pictures to show what work your parents do.

My mother is a _____.	My father is a _____.

6 Circle the correct ending for each of the sentences.

The person in the picture is a ...

a doctor

b teacher

c bus driver

d hairdresser

The person in the picture is a ...

a teacher

b police officer

c mechanic

d barber

7 Use words from the box to fill in the gaps.

plants	useful	water
people	around	animals

a Resources are _____ things.

b Resources are all _____ us.

c Plants, _____ and _____ are examples of resources.

d Our most important resource is _____.

8 Circle all the things water is used for.

cooking

washing

bathing

jumping

drinking

skipping

9 Draw pictures in the boxes to show FOUR things we use the land for.

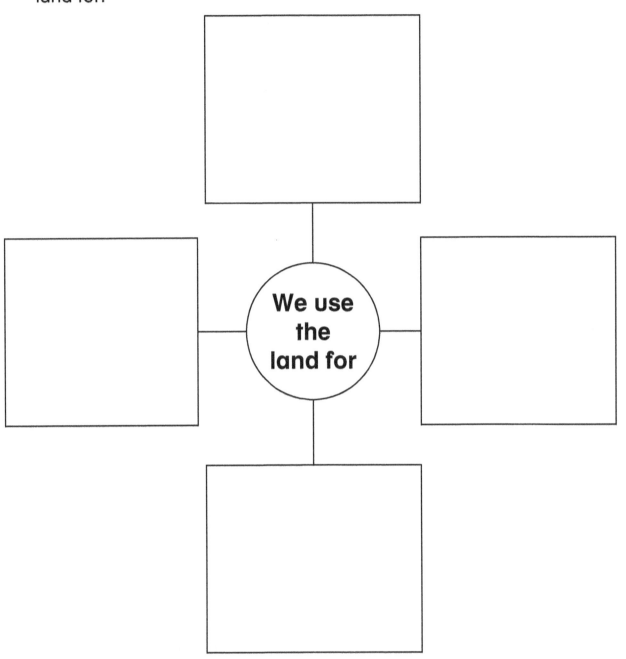

We use
the
land for

10 Look at the pictures and their labels. Do they come from plants or animals? Draw a line from each one to either PLANT or ANIMAL.

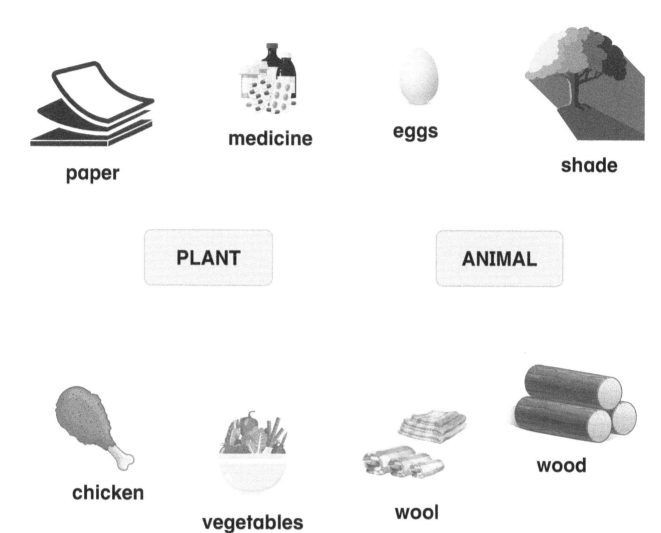

paper

medicine

eggs

shade

PLANT

ANIMAL

chicken

vegetables

wool

wood

11 Complete the sentence in the box.

Goods are things that we can _____ and _____.

Find pictures of goods and paste them in the box below. Write the name of each one.

_____	_____
_____	_____
_____	_____

12 Match each worker to the goods that they produce. Draw lines.

Worker	Goods
farmer	cake
baker	clothes
fisherman	fish
tailor	house
chef	vegetables
carpenter	bread

13 Who am I ?

These workers all provide a service. Read what service the workers provide and write the correct worker's name on the line. Choose from the names in the box.

Teacher	**Dentist**	**Doctor**
Policeman	**Taxi-driver**	**Crossing guard**

a I help you when you are sick. Who am I? _____

b I help you to cross the road safely. Who am I? _____

c I help you to learn at school. Who am I? _____

d I protect you from harm and danger. Who am I? _____

e I take care of your teeth. Who am I? _____

f I get you to places you want to go. Who am I? _____

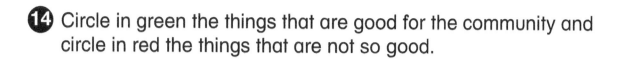

14 Circle in green the things that are good for the community and circle in red the things that are not so good.

Cutting down trees

Planting flowers

Throwing garbage
on the floor

Putting garbage
in a bin

15 Find the words in the puzzle.

ANIMALS   PLANTS

GOODS   PRODUCE

LAND   RESOURCE

NEEDS   SERVICES

PEOPLE   WORKERS

E	V	N	L	N	P	W	S	F	Y
Z	C	A	E	L	O	E	X	D	Z
O	N	E	A	R	C	H	W	J	A
D	D	N	K	I	M	X	O	O	K
S	T	E	V	P	E	O	P	L	E
S	R	R	P	R	O	D	U	C	E
S	E	R	E	S	O	U	R	C	E
S	A	N	I	M	A	L	S	N	P
W	M	P	S	S	D	O	O	G	T
M	X	J	H	Q	R	R	U	C	M

4 Leaders

Student's Book pages 44–49

1 Write the names of the groups you belong to in the box.

_____

_____

_____

_____

_____

_____

2 Put these leaders in the correct part of the table below.

pastor   teacher   mother

principal   father   prime minister

Home	School	Community

3 Find pictures of these leaders of Antigua and Barbuda. Stick one in each box. Write their names below.

The Governor General   The Leader of the Opposition   The Prime Minister

_____   _____   _____

_____   _____   _____

4 Which picture shows children who are following rules? Draw a circle around it.

5 Which are school rules and which are not school rules? Read these rules and decide if they would be good for your school. Put a ✓ in the box if it's good and a ✗ if it's not good.

Run in school. ☐

Keep the classroom tidy. ☐

Always do your best. ☐

Be rude to teachers. ☐

You must make lots of noise in class. ☐

Arrive at school on time. ☐

Put your hand up in class if you want to say something. ☐

Don't bother to help other children. ☐

6 What do good leaders do? Put a ✓ or a ✗ in the box beside each one. A ✓ means a good leader does this. A ✗ means they don't.

Encourage members of the group to work together.

☐

Make decisions.

☐

Organise things.

☐

Encourage members of the group not to follow rules.

☐

Sit back and let everyone else work.

☐

Make sure rules are followed.

☐

Encourage members of the group to try their best.

☐

7 Fill in the diagram with four of the rules you have in your family.

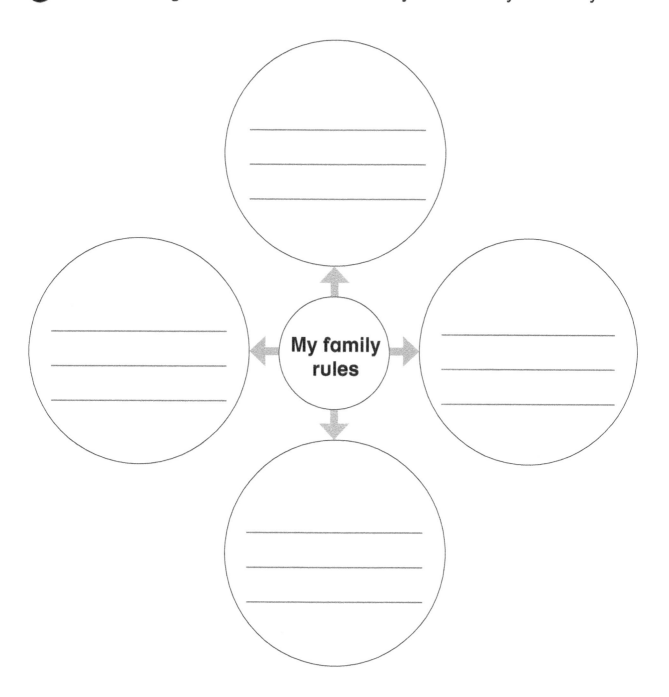

8 Circle the pictures that show children behaving well in the classroom.

9 Find these words in the puzzle.

BEHAVIOUR   ORDER

FOLLOW   PARENTS

GROUPS   PRINCIPAL

LEADERS   RESPECT

OBEY   RULES

W	O	L	L	O	F	L	S	B	P
R	L	V	N	J	R	A	P	E	A
U	R	D	S	E	T	P	U	H	R
L	P	U	D	P	C	I	O	A	E
E	G	R	N	M	E	C	R	V	N
S	O	K	N	Y	P	N	G	I	T
Y	E	B	O	Y	S	I	H	O	S
K	W	O	I	T	E	R	R	U	Y
C	W	F	A	C	R	P	J	R	K
O	I	S	R	E	D	A	E	L	H

5 Safety

Student's Book pages 50–55

1 Use words from the box to fill in the gaps in the sentences below.

> obey   accident   safe   rules

a We have _____ for travelling.

b We must _____ travel rules.

c They help to keep us _____ .

d People who do not obey safety rules may have an

_____ .

2 Answer these questions.

a What side of the road do we drive on in Antigua?

_____

b Which way should we look just before stepping out to cross the road?

_____

3 Put a ✓ in the box next to the pictures which show children obeying traffic rules and a ✗ in the box next to the pictures which show children NOT obeying traffic rules.

4 Are these safety rules for walking, driving or playing?

Write **Walking**, **Driving** or **Playing**.

a Sit down at all times. _____

b Play fairly. _____

c Walk at the side of the road. _____

d Wear your seatbelt at all times. _____

e Don't play near the road. _____

f Wait for the green 'walk' sign before crossing the road. _____

5 Match the traffic signs with their meanings.

                    Speed limit

                    No entry

                    No right turn

                    Traffic light

                    Pedestrian crossing

                    No left turn

                    School ahead

6 Colour in the traffic light with the correct colours.

Red means _____

Green means _____

7 Find these words in the puzzle.

ACCIDENT   SAFETY
DANGER   SIGNS
DRIVE   STOP
HARM   TRAFFIC
PLAY   WALK

A	R	E	G	N	A	D	S	S	H
U	C	C	R	U	P	S	A	T	A
R	A	C	L	M	I	K	F	O	R
R	G	D	I	G	S	T	E	P	M
I	W	X	N	D	R	R	T	X	H
O	M	S	R	A	E	L	Y	E	Q
O	Q	K	F	U	N	N	X	V	K
Q	Q	F	W	A	L	K	T	I	S
O	I	Y	A	L	P	L	M	R	M
C	O	T	U	A	R	I	Q	D	H

6 Moving about

Student's Book pages 56–63

1 In the box, write the names of some of the places that you go to in your neighbourhood.

2 Look at the map of the neighbourhood and complete the sentences below.

a The church is near to the _____ .

b The shop is left of the _____ .

c The police station is right of the _____ .

d The school is a long way from the _____ .

3 Label the points of the compass correctly.

West   East   North   South

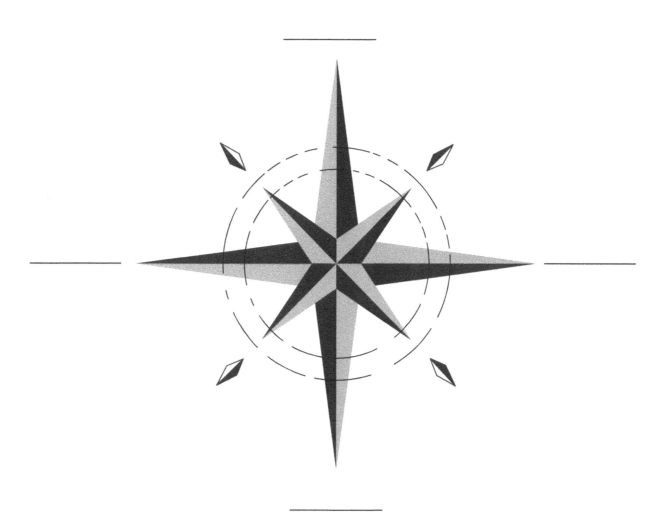

4 Look at the map of Barbuda. Use the compass points to give the location of these places.

a The lagoon is north of _____ .

b The Martello Tower is west of _____ .

c The Highlands is _____ of Darby's Cave.

d Darby's Cave is _____ of the lagoon.

5 Look at these pictures of different types of transport. Are they land, sea or air? Draw lines to link each one to the correct word in a box.

Air

Land

Sea

6 Which sort of transportation would you use for each of the following?

Write **Land**, **Sea** or **Air**.

1. Going to the supermarket. _____

2. Going to Dominica. _____

3. Going on a cruise _____

7 Draw a line to link each transportation centre with the correct transport.

Harbour

Airport

Bus station

8 Role-play

Work in groups of four. Read the text and then plan how you can act it out in your group.

> Jay and his family are planning a trip to Barbuda next week to visit the Bird Sanctuary. They live in Jennings.
>
> They need to decide how they are going to travel. They don't have a car.

Role-play a family discussion to decide on the modes of transportation the family will need to use. You will each be one member of the family.

The pictures below will help you.

9 Find these words in the puzzle.

AIR	SEA
BICYCLE	TAXI
BUS	TRANSPORT
HELICOPTER	TRAVEL
LAND	TRUCK

U	Y	T	I	F	B	E	L	Y	O
P	E	R	A	U	T	L	E	X	A
M	R	A	S	R	G	C	V	K	D
P	P	N	H	E	A	Y	A	T	S
M	X	S	T	I	L	C	R	J	T
T	R	P	R	P	H	I	T	R	D
A	N	O	F	M	I	B	U	N	U
X	T	R	D	S	Y	C	A	V	S
I	X	T	T	C	K	L	A	E	S
H	E	L	I	C	O	P	T	E	R

7 Communication

Student's Book pages 64–71

1 Use words from the box to fill in the gaps in the sentences.

feel	share	receiving	people
talking	body	frowning	smiling

a We communicate with other _____.

b Communication is sending and _____ messages.

c We communicate to say how we _____.

d We communicate to _____ ideas.

e We communicate most often by _____ .

f We also use _____ language to communicate,

by _____ or _____ , for example.

2 How many ways of communicating can you think of? Add as many as you can to this mind map.

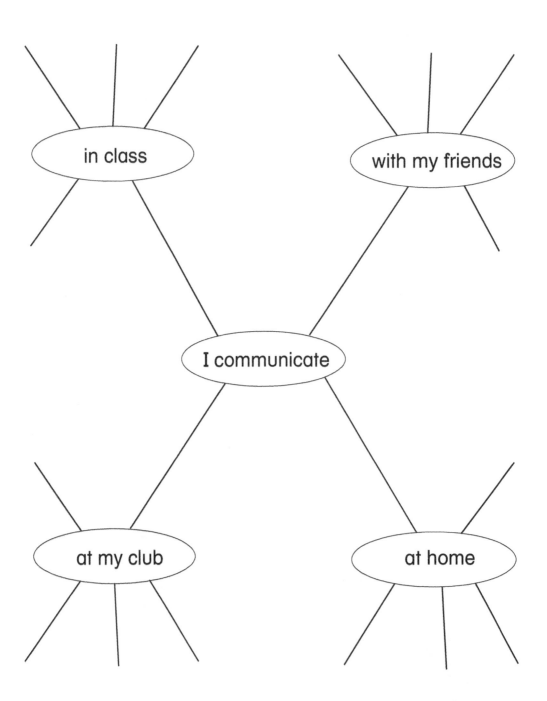

3 What do these emojis show? Write the emotion each one is communicating. Choose from the box.

angry	sad	happy	very upset

_____   _____

_____   _____

4 Circle all the things we use to communicate with other people.

5 Answer your classmates' questions about the communication instruments below.

Kimmie: What is this ?

You: It is a _____.

Marcia: What is this?

You: It is a _____.

Vernicia : What is this?

You: It is a _____.

Zuri: What is this?

You: It is a _____.

6 Finish each of these sentences. The pictures in the box will help you.

a To send a letter, I would go to a _____.

b To listen to the weather forecast, I would use a _____.

c To ring a friend, I would use a _____.

d To send an email, I would use a _____.

7 Read the invitation to a party, then answer the questions below.

> Please come to my birthday party on Saturday.
>
> It is at Sunset Beach at 3 o'clock.
>
> We can swim and have fun.
>
> From Izzy

a What day is the party on? _____

b What is the name of the beach? _____

c What time is the party? _____

d What will they do at the party? _____

e Whose party is it? _____

8 Find a piece of visual communication you like or think works very well. It might be a poster at school, an advert in the street, something in a shop – the choice is yours. Copy it in the box below.

Or you could make up your own!

9 Find these words in the puzzle.

EMAIL

FROWN

INTERNET

LANGUAGE

LETTER

NEWSPAPER

RADIO

SMILE

SYMBOLS

TELEPHONE

O	M	R	E	T	T	E	L	P	T
Z	M	A	O	Z	I	I	F	K	E
H	V	M	C	B	J	U	R	L	N
R	A	D	I	O	U	V	O	P	R
S	Y	M	B	O	L	S	W	D	E
S	M	I	L	E	T	E	N	F	T
R	E	P	A	P	S	W	E	N	N
E	N	O	H	P	E	L	E	T	I
R	B	E	M	A	I	L	P	E	K
L	A	N	G	U	A	G	E	L	G

Notes

Notes

Notes

Notes

Notes

Notes

Notes